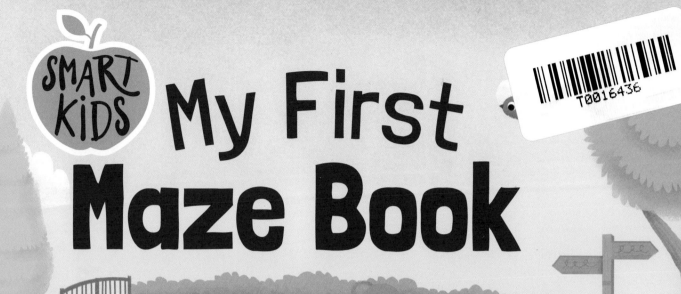

SMART KIDS
My First Maze Book

ARCTURUS

This edition published in 2022 by Arcturus Publishing Limited
26/27 Bickels Yard, 151–153 Bermondsey Street,
London SE1 3HA

Author: Lisa Regan
Illustrator: Kate Daubney
Editor: Violet Peto
Designer: Nathan Balsom
Managing Editor: Joe Harris
Design Manager: Jessica Holliland

ISBN: 978-1-3988-2029-6
CH010428NT
Supplier 29, Date 0822, PI 00002199

Printed in China

Dinosaur Dash

Can you find the safest path for the baby dinosaur to take to reach its home?

START →

↓
FINISH

Sports Day

Be the fastest through the maze and claim your medal!

START

FINISH

Ride the Rapids

Hold on tight! See if you can make it through the rushing water to the end!

START

FINISH

Pirate Puzzle

Can you guide Cap'n Cat from the pirate ship to the buried treasure?

START

FINISH

Wiggly Worms

Which of the wiggly worms can reach the
food stored in the middle of the tunnels?

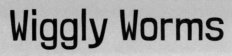

FINISH

Happy Birds

Help the happy birds get past the obstacles to reach their nest.

START

FINISH

Amazing Ocean

Ride the right water bubbles to guide the
turtle safely to the coral reef.

START

FINISH

Modern Art

Guide Pablo Pigasso along the correct paint path
to his easel, so he can create a masterpiece.

FINISH

Nutty Navigator

Quick! Help Sorcha Squirrel find her buried nuts before Charlie Chipmunk can get his claws on them.

START

FINISH

All Aboard!

See how quickly Masato Macaque can get the top-speed train from station to station.

START

FINISH

14

A Walk in the Woods

Follow the footprints to help Deborah Deer
find her way home.

START

FINISH

At the Building Site

Help the road roller flatten a path from one side
of the construction site to the other.

START

FINISH

Fairytale Fun

Help the prince find a route across
the pond to the princess.

START

FINISH

Super Yummy

Can you find a way through the strawberry sauce that goes all the way from the top to the cherry at the bottom of the glass?

START

FINISH

On Your Bike!

This cycle path has some amazing ramps! Trace the route fast enough to jump over the gaps as you race to the finish line.

START

FINISH

Monkey Maze

Help Missy Monkey swing through the trees to reach the delicious fruit.

START

FINISH

Haunted House

Help the ghost find a way from the ground floor to the attic, so it can get some rest.

FINISH

START

Bumper Cars

Help Rasheed Rooster drive the number 4 dodgem from the purple flag to the yellow flag without hitting any obstacles along the way!

START

FINISH

Shooting Stars

Wish upon a star and try to find a path from one
shooting star to the other. So beautiful!

START

FINISH

Monster Mash

Lottie Llama is sleepwalking again! Guide her safely back to bed without crashing into any monsters along the way!

FINISH

START

Rainy Days

Find a way to get from the bus to the house. Be sure to jump in all the puddles in between!

START

FINISH

Escape Route

How did the genie get out of the bottle to freedom?

FINISH

START

Snow Days

Follow the footprints in the snow. Which
of the snow figures did each owl make?

Beep Beep!

Find a way for Liam Lion to get to the superstore.
Watch out for dead ends!

START

FINISH

Blast Off!

Follow the rocket on its route around the planets.
Which of the planets does it miss?

START

FINISH

To the Rescue!

Firefighter Fiona needs to get to the cat stuck in the tree as fast as she can. Can you guide her?

START →

FINISH

Splash!

Whiz your way from the top to the bottom of the world's most amazing water slide!

START

FINISH

34

Rabbit Run

It's bedtime for these baby bunnies. Help them find their way to their bedroom.

START

FINISH

Fancy Footwork

Help Sammy Skunk dribble the ball all the way to the goal.

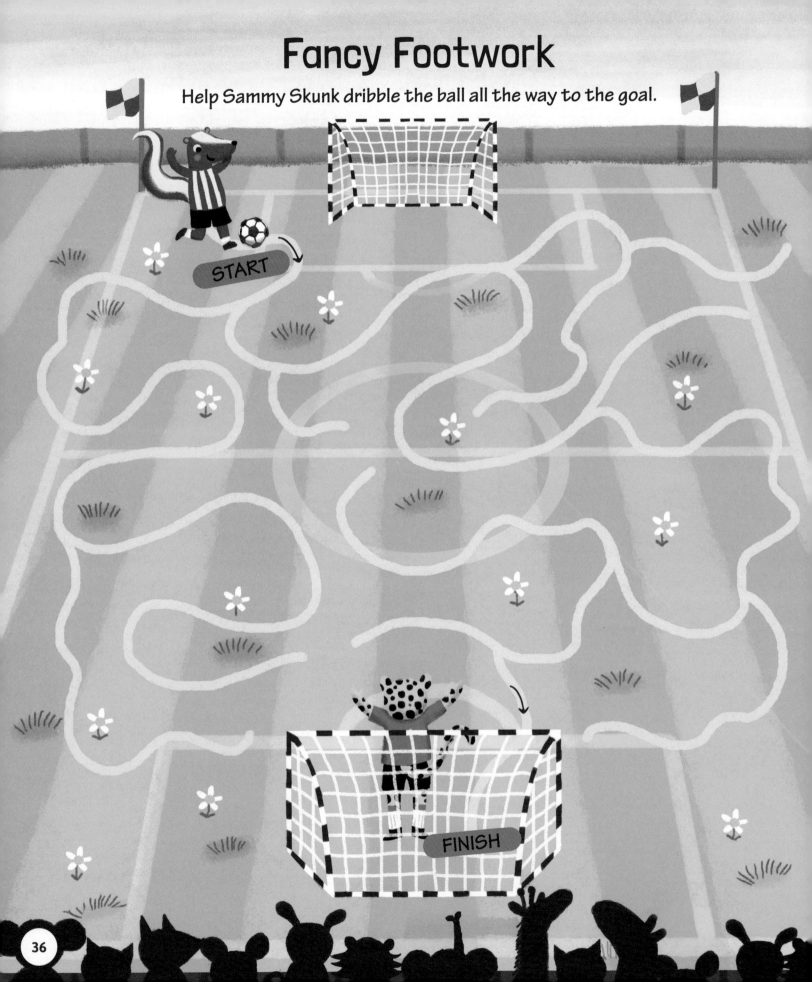

START

FINISH

High on a Hill

Gabriel Goat has lost his flock!
Can you help him find them?

FINISH

START

Bathtime Bubbles

Have some foamy fun finding a way from one side
of the tub to the other.

START

FINISH

Takeout Treats

Which of the pathways has all of the toppings needed for the finished pizza?

START

FINISH

All the Balls

It's soft-play time! Find a way out of the ball pit so Kylie Kitten can grab a much-needed drink.

START

FINISH

Down in the Deep

Help both sea otters find their way through
the sea kelp to the sea urchins.

START

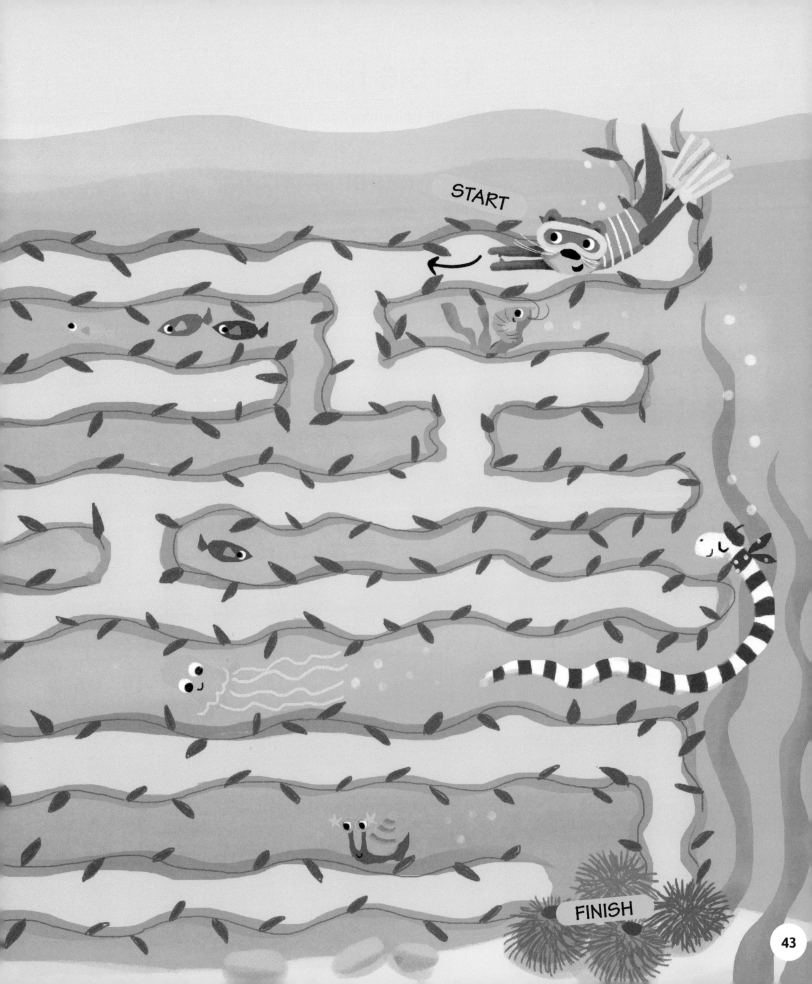

START

FINISH

43

Marble Run

Which route will take the marble all the way down to the jar at the bottom?

START

FINISH

The Clock Strikes Twelve

Help the prince find his true love
to return her lost slipper.

START

FINISH

So Hungry

Wiggle Worm has a mighty appetite! Find a path from cupcake to cupcake and see how many treats he has eaten along the way!

START

FINISH

One Shoe Two Shoe

Red shoe, blue shoe! Help Olaf and Olin find their lost shoes.

START

FINISH

Pony Parade

Help Pablo Pony ride around the correct jump course to win the golden cup.

START

FINISH

Festival Fun

Welcome to the Dragon Boat Festival! Can you see a clear way for the yellow team to catch up with the red team?

START

FINISH

High in the Sky

Which of the loop-the-loops takes the plane safely back to the airfield?

FINISH

I Need a Hug

Benjamin Bear is feeling fed up. Guide him along the correct path to find his parents to cheer him up.

START

FINISH

Party Animals

These meerkats love a party! Find a way from the entrance to the amazing cake and LET'S DANCE!

FINISH

START

Treasure Trail

Help Kamala Kangaroo stash some cash in her pouch to deposit safely in the bank. How many coins will she collect as she hops her way to the finish?

START

FINISH

Ice Ice Baby

Which route will take Nils Narwhal back to the rest of his pod?

START

FINISH

Enchanted Kingdom

Guide the prince through the kingdom to find the princess in her magical garden.

START

FINISH

Eat, Sleep, Repeat

Snoozy Susie the koala is exhausted! Help her
find her way to the comfortable branch for a nap.

START

FINISH

A Fast Finish

Help Chibuzo race back to her cubs.
Which route is the shortest and quickest?

FINISH

START

Camping Trip

Chico needs to get back to his empty tent, and he has to brush his teeth on the way, so he's ready for bedtime. Don't get the wrong tent!

START

FINISH

61

Clowning Around

Find a way from start to finish to claim a prize at the end.

Home Run

Help Brad Beaver run to home base without running into any of his opponents.

FINISH

24 5 3 6

START

Behind the Scenes

Paloma has stage fright! Guide her through the maze to take her place on the stage where she belongs.

START

FINISH

Silly Billy!

Silly Billy Baboon has left his boxing boots at home.
Quickly find a route back home for him to collect them.

START

FINISH

Lemurs Love Lemons!

Help Lucky and Lucia bound around and join their friends
by following a path that only has lemons on it.

START

FINISH

The Clean Team

Will Jojo take a bath or have a shower? See which one she goes past on her way to get dry and warm again.

START

FINISH

Lost Property

Poor baby pangolin has dropped her teddy bear on the way home from the store. Help mother pangolin retrace their steps to find it.

START

FINISH

Feeling Peckish?

Guide the hens back to the hen house. They might even get a few snacks along the way!

START

FINISH

Bear Hunt!

The bears are going on a hunt! See if they can find a way through all the obstacles to get to the cave at the end.

START

FINISH

Traffic Jam

Follow the rows and rows of traffic
to find a way over the bridge.

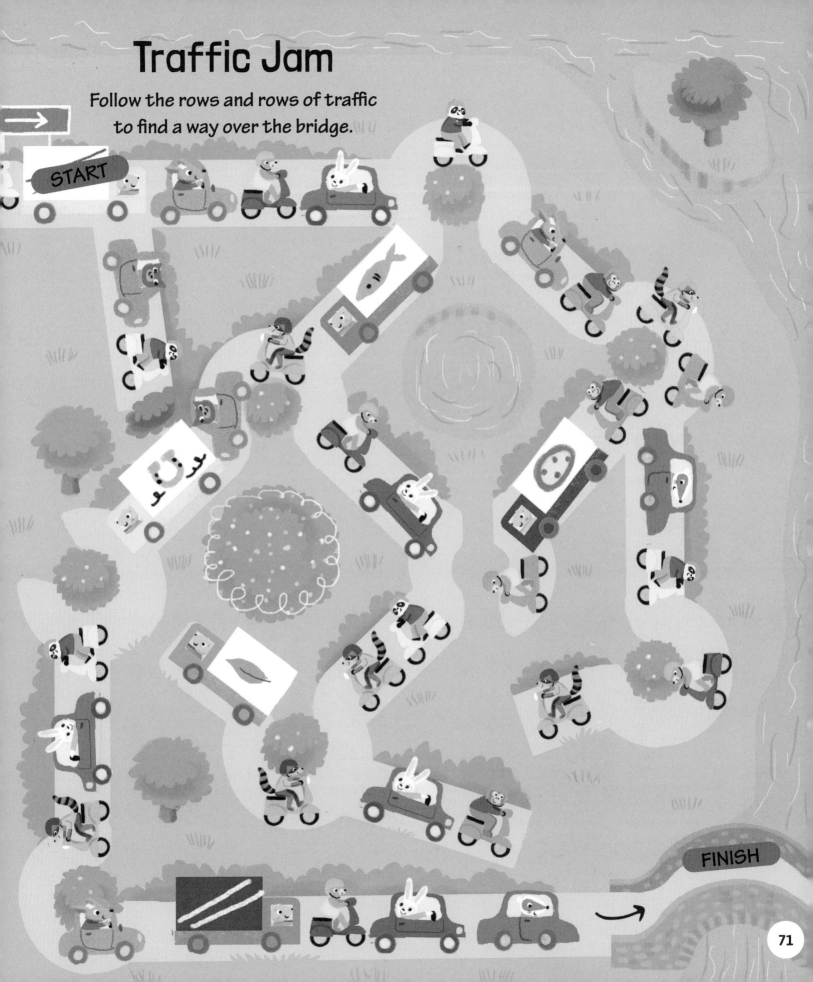

START

FINISH

Spaghetti Betty

Betty's spaghetti is going everywhere!
Have fun finding a way from her plate to her mouth.

START

FINISH

Sea Queen

Help HRH Orla the orca swim back to her royal throne as fast as she can.

START

FINISH

Tiger Tennis

Anyone for tennis? Fatima is ready to play; she just needs to get there. Give her a helping hand.

START

FINISH

74

Water Babies

Guide the hippos along the marshes
and then into the river.

START

FINISH

Spotted!

Have fun with Julian Jaguar by working your way through the dots and spots to get to the finish.

START

FINISH

Man Overboard!

Saju Shark has spotted a sudden splash in the water. Help him swim through the waves to see what's happening by the boat.

START

FINISH

Messy Pups

Uh-oh! These rally drivers have got to get past some sticky mud. Guide all of them safely to the finish line.

FINISH

START

78

1-2-3-BLOW!

What made the pufferfish blow up? Find the correct path from start to finish to see what was so scary.

START

FINISH

Jungle Jazz

Sonny the gorilla needs to put in some music practice.
Can you guide him back to his drum kit?

START

FINISH

Dive! Dive!

Find a way for the submarine to travel through the depths of the ocean to explore the shipwreck.

START

FINISH

Feeding Frenzy

Ritchie Raccoon is preparing for a long winter. How many tasty treats does he find on his way back to his den?

START

FINISH

Time for Bed

Before lights out, help Antonio Anteater find a way
through the piles of books so he can climb into bed.

START

FINISH

Answers

Page 3

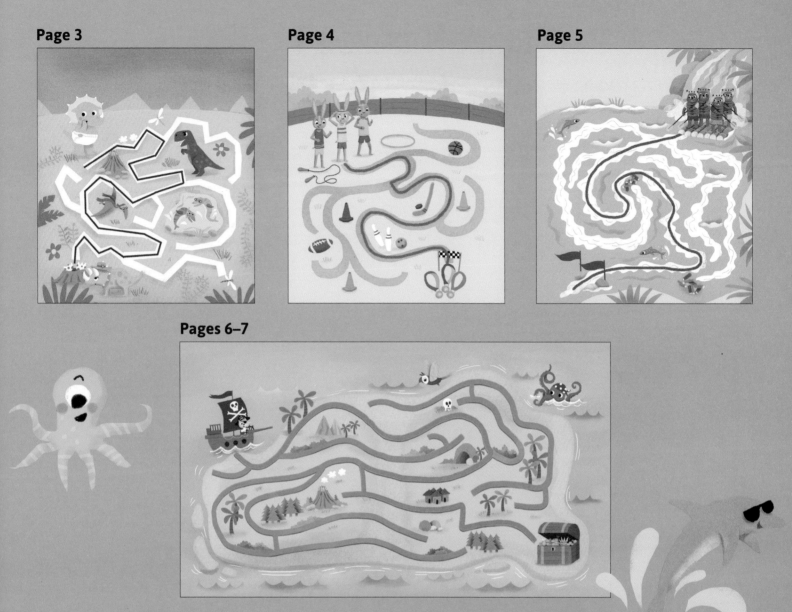

Page 4

Page 5

Pages 6–7

Page 8

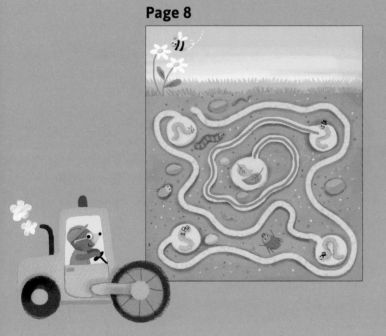

Page 9

Pages 10–11

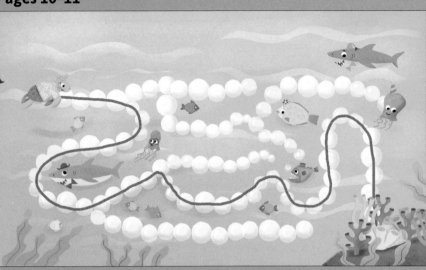

Page 12

Page 13

Page 14

Page 15

Pages 16–17

Page 18

Page 19

Page 20

Page 21

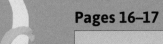

87

Page 22

Page 23

Page 24

Page 25

Pages 26–27

Page 28

Page 29

Page 30

Page 31

Pages 32–33

Page 34

Page 35

Page 36

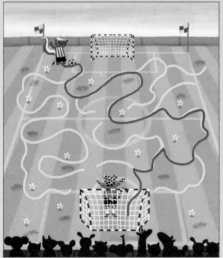

Page 37

Pages 38–39

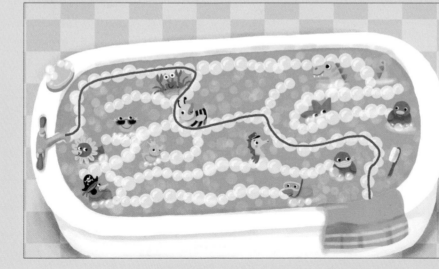

Page 40

Page 41

Pages 42–43

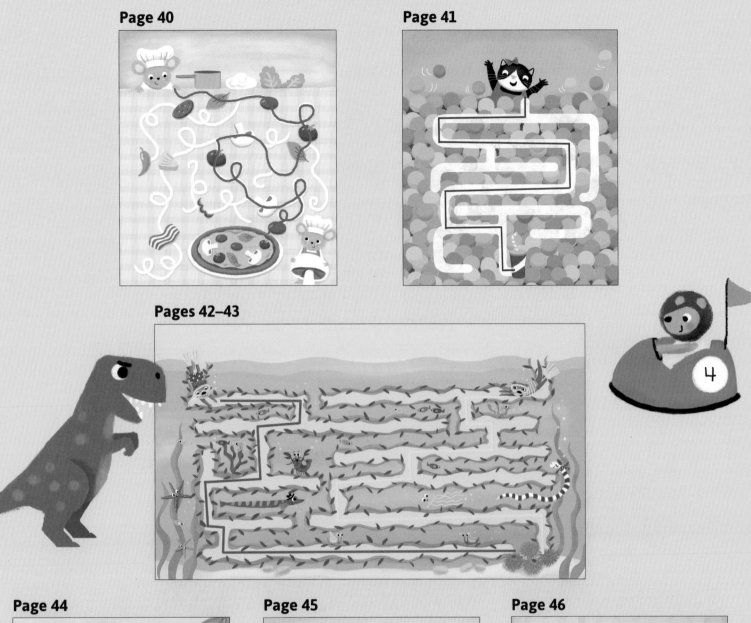

Page 44

Page 45

Page 46

Page 47

Page 48

Page 49

Pages 50–51

Page 52

Page 53

Page 54

29 coins

Page 55

Pages 56–57

Page 58

Page 59

Pages 60–61

Page 62

Page 63

Page 64

Page 65

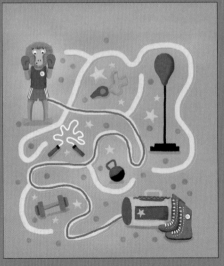

Page 66

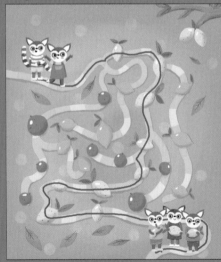

Page 67

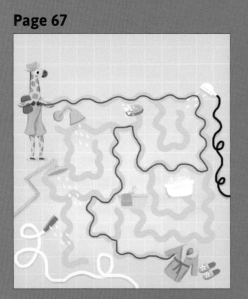

Page 68

Page 69

Page 70

Page 71

Page 72

Page 73

Page 74

Page 75

Page 76

Page 77

Page 78

Page 79

Page 80

Page 81

Page 82

6 treats

Page 83